If we are the forest the animals dream

If we are the forest the animals dream

Patrick Cahill

SIXTEEN RIVERS PRESS

Printed in the United States of America

Published by Sixteen Rivers Press
P.O. Box 640663
San Francisco, CA 94164-0663
sixteenrivers.org

LCCN: 2024952891
ISBN: 978-1-939639-41-7

Cover painting: *From the Balcony, Pinecrest, Tuolumne County,* by Eileen Downey
Cover design: Brendan Cahill
Author photo: Art Bodner
Book design: Wayne Smith

In memory of my sister,

Sara Cahill

Contents

THREE

FOUR

FIVE

ONE

Fue bello vivir
Cuando vivias!

It was beautiful to live
When you lived!

—Pablo Neruda, "Finale"

Dear Sara

Remember that footbridge in Mexico, the one we used to cross on our way to La Peñita? You were wary of the bridge, not because of the alligator we were told lived in the reeds just below, but because of its suspended sway. You didn't much care for its height, either, though it wasn't *that* high. But anyway, you crossed it. I've turned that bridge into language, given it substance in another world—that's what we do. Oh, I know, the bridge will doubtless outlast us, the words and us. But while they last, they *will* create bridges in the mind, and in the bodies of those able to feel its sway. *Remember.* A word that becomes more significant as significance deserts us. I see you still at the end of the bridge, that look in your eye, uneasy but determined, looking in my direction, preparing to cross.

Yours as always

Departure

Kingston   Port Gamble   Hood Canal   Discovery Bay
to Old Fort Townsend   Protection Island   S'Klallam
Sequim (rhymes with swim)   white chop against the
bridge   rain pixelated the windshield   shimmered
temperature dropped   the river Elwha   something to
remember   the last ferry over   have you forgotten it all

Looking for the Car

We walked up what
61st off Alki
back from the beach
the five of us alcohol
nudging us through the dark
misleading streets
the sky breathless everywhere
in fragments
trees tracing the black air
we left back where

wind had whipped your ashes
over the water across the rocks
and concrete steps
into our hearts
into the salt washed air we breathed

Fable

El puente es tuyo

This is the way you enter the place

why

because the footbridge is yours

why

because it calls you here to feel its sway

why

because you were found among the stars

so

the stars became a storm became a snow a scrim

a screen of water a sheet of air

and

an alligator waits for you beneath the bridge

why

because beneath his memory lurks a winter gaze

and

he has a voice a second voice for you

go on

as light falls across the reeds and warms his blood

isn't there another way

no

will it console him

what

my second voice

you will never know

or bring me to his jaws

till you cross the bridge the swaying bridge

you will never know

TWO

And since time sets its own tempo, like a heartbeat or an ebb tide, timepieces don't really keep time. They just keep up with it, if they're able.

—Dava Sobel, from *Longitude*

Isfahan

a touch of perfume inside her wrist   carries the scent
    of longing and loss   a distant then   *how do I take that*
mountain where I go   *where you go it goes*   a lemon tree
    at the top of the stairs   Billy Strayhorn's "Isfahan" composing
the street

    fragrance in the air   evening on the pittosporum
dreaming in slow motion   *Isfahan is half of the world*

    slid the flat blade of the knife   across her tongue
savored the lemon juice it left   ice melted in the palm
    of her words   that spider in the clock   last seen
weaving its time   the invisible city of Isfahan

Frequencies

The tower's vertiginous wooden frame   rises
above the plain   a glacial plateau rising just beyond
and above   Coteau des Prairies   among whose sloughs
and shallow lakes she dug a six-foot cubicle   a home
underground   a home in a hole   prairie roots   its walls
frost late in autumn   coyote rodent deer peered in
night's decapitations   did she enter their dreams
did they hers   lost to us   distant and invisible from
the tower   though nothing is lost   above the hole above
the tower   air shifting into higher frequencies of blue

What are you looking for

a border to cross?   I'm looking for borders
to cross   urgent fierce borders   along impulsive
rivers   smoldering lines of demarcation   incinerated
borders   in the glaring interstices of shattered glass
in the shards of our reflection   little explosions   against
the surface of the eye   in the just invisible pattern
a shotgun leaves in the air   within those ad-libbed spaces
you play among   that left-hand stride   will you listen
its rhythm   where the wind lets loose   tremors
in the sky

Horses in Truck

Branches caught up above the traffic's commotion
flailing in its movement   between the nicotine and
Benzedrine   will you arrive in snow time   an empty rig
in a driveway—*HORSES IN TRUCK*   road gravel gathering up
longitude and ice   the barn giving way

or yellow roses beside the horse   the apple tree gone
white   momentum in a lingering embrace   relentless in
its consummation   a router's moans   moving across the
wind   dirt demons rummaging the furrows   after
stubble the plow redd up   the half-life of memory

Ashes

after David Maisel's photographs in Library of Dust

A drifter's Appaloosa swims upstream, past the confinement of the mentally fraught, whose ashes dust the interiors of rusted metal boxes, cubes arranged beside the abandoned asylum, where skulls were often made of glass, their empty eyes holding a reflection of empty rooms, passes a green strip, a fence and furrowed field, the wind blowing inside a clock, as flies bite the Appaloosa's emerging coat leaving the stream, a minor event among the reeds, just beyond the margins of our perception, the drifter a thief who couldn't know when he would finally take the hook that pulls him under.

Trek

Escarpment rising through windswept terminology   flat
snow or layered sun   wildings' spoor   swept away
to stream view after the dissolve   on which we glide
hanging growth   blades roiling the wet shade   whose
patterns we devise   the water's surface slipping past
the faint swirl our tracks

Saddle Up

Rustler Anne underneath a broad-brimmed black hat
she's on her way to some café   or cool saloon   the hat
raked just right   with a little sass   she crosses invisible
borders   still with Johnny-come-lately   no desperado
Dan   no giddyup and go   salsa sauce mustard crisp on
a missing tie   a string tie   light rain the street lamp's
yellow   light contriving its puddle of stars   glinting on
the dark wet walk   so what's your plan   that scent of
whiskey   loitering on the breath you share   with
Johnny-come   what do you rustle now R Anne   some
gray forms just visible in a snowstorm   come summer
distant indistinct in the trembling heat   the narrative
pulling you in   or under   you feel the fall into winter
days   your deciduous smile fading   with summer light
remember when Doc Watson   brought tears to your eyes

Birds

Just outside my window
the tree draws the scrub jay
into its interior
absorbs it

Other animals wander inside
a beast we've yet to imagine

The streetcar eases in
afloat on its insistent whine

The small girl across from me
lifts her hand
weaves an inscription across the air
an infinity symbol   an ampersand
or proofreader's delete

A dark tide moves across the earth
shape shifting   elusive

A mud hen's shadow
among the reeds

An imagined gunshot's
transparency

Lerici

Shelley looks up
scans the blue contusions
above the Bay of Lerici
for orbital debris

What Life Is This

clouds burnt an oppressive orange
        steel-engraved horizon

some relic in the fore-life
        accumulating artifacts

or where you've been
        an obscure wood
slipping definition

  under the jacaranda
        perplexed among forgotten words

you leaning over a wooden fence
        into the heat of summer
 rising from a garden

let us build our small stages
        our little boxes

among whose gathered objects our mirrored
        selves can live

There's No One Here

Sip a cocktail on the Boulevard de la Bastille
sun bleaching the promenade

that wan look that shadows your face
as though something has been erased

a mist of animals gone by the window
snow flurries melting in April air

you can never have too much
unpredictable weather

blue drifted the flax field once
colored the page

a murder not of crows this time
but monsters

slow your pace without slipping
into the past

while some conspiratorial urge
fells the woods

or as they say in the Company
let's go dark

Navigation

Windows migrate   symmetrical   exhausting
inexhaustible   shadows drop   buildings blank   he
enters his moving shadow cast before him on the walk
disappears into it   is this a map

Roads cross   city a gray conjecture   flowing green
advances   above a field   moisture   toward an
orange surface burn   wind streaks   a blue expanse
undisturbed of consequence as sunlight falls   a white
patch   island or cloud   something erased   varied
unvaried curvatures of blue

Cross section   radial lines radiating upward into an
expanding airless arch   downward core bound toward
an imperceptible   constant   rumored convergence

Spilled ink migrates along the fabric's fibers   through
its weave   a black cloud obliterating fanciful lines
shadings   ticks

The cartographer distracted   astigmatic   arthritic   lame
retains his position—though how, one wonders—takes up
his much-loved instruments   begins again

Doubt

She fled the crime scene, unclothed, a killer. We tracked her through woodland, we tracked her through thickets, but she absorbed the light as she fled. Mosquito grit rose in her wake. Perfume, sweat, cuts, insects her clothing now. Wind swept back from a river she sought a deletion in her flight. Our flashlights' yellow probes passed over the undergrowth. We moved through shadows—our memory house—eaves an eruption of blood into the dusk, dragon scales a thicket of birds silent in their flight, our victim's wound a sheath for her abandoned knife clotted with motive, recollection, the past. Will she vanish in the water's rush as we go on, free of mirrors, its dark surface her reflection now, her lacerations a diagram of these events? Will we go on, follow the river downstream along its bank, find comfort in its ceaseless, indifferent noise, or upstream toward a puzzle of uncertain intent?

Flood

They sat up high on the roof, the two of them,
the water below swallowing their words

A woman, just a level down, stood at a window
a white hibiscus in her hair

hesitated, then jumped
into a tree

A breeze hummed in the blinds that she left behind
Another woman, one remembered, never believed

getting off in the front seat impossible,
rain battering the car's roof

Did the woman in the tree laugh
or was it just the ache of drifting debris

The sky shifted a bit to the left
scrambled its reflection

unhinged the invisible
streets below

They breathed in the flooding waste's aroma
the treetop now arousing the wind

The word *weather* eludes me, the other one thought
It sounds like *whether,* now an inescapable choice

whether to weather the rising flood
or jump into what's left of the tree

It began to rain, a hard rain graying the world's features
Is that the woman still hidden among the leaves

or a bobcat, they thought
Is that the tree even, or a trick of the rain

the implausible world, woman roof and tree
dissolving in the summer air

If I wake up falling

sideways out of a chair
If I walk through a vertical rain
If I am the wind settling on an empty shed
If I am a starling shaking off water
in puddled grass
If I am the mist falling through sunlight
If I am a note endlessly struck on the dog-eared air
If I am the man twitching on the corner
If I am the current coursing through his body
If I am the deadliest animal on earth
setting toxins adrift in his blood
If I am the dead drawing his spirit into our remains
If I am the startled security guard
and the bullet freeing the blood sequestered in his flesh
If I am the blood
If I am the flesh
If I am not the reflection in the mirror
If I am the Blood Wolf Moon howling back at the many reflections
of what I am
If I am your swagger walking down the street
or a tinfoil wind flashing the multiple images of what we are
If I am the psalm and you are the song
If I am the force field and you are the force
If we are the forest the animals dream

THREE

"I am a silent echo of the elements"
—Antonin Dvořák, *Rusalka*

Frogs in the Basement

The water in disarray, yet you pack that basket filled with wind through waves of light, the wind's salt left in your hair. As though that sparrow could merge its ghost's transparency with some feathered image and fly away. Its blood as satin as our blood, burn marked, rain raw. The words we've kidnapped thundering in the basement stroll through every consequence as autumn drains away. Are those tentacles in your teeth, a taste of brine, lips in motion? We've taken reality apart, spit in its eye, and put it back together again, a nose here, an eyelash in the leaves, tongue—leftovers dropped in a pouch. So what if the future is approaching, outbound and crowded, standing room only—well then, we'll stand.

To the Water's Edge

I set myself on fire again, deposit the gathering ashes in a mold, my shadow dancing them around the rim. The shadow I meant to wash away at memory's end, turn off the light under our skin. You fill a pillbox with love's complaints in wet black ink, smeared across the glow. You were always good at swallowing the rain. We had a drink on the lady seated just to our left. Added layers until we were ripe, overripe. A decline into yeast, she pointed out. We want to be contained. Our thoughts were always invisible till they struck whatever, a hammered copper bowl, a tusk. The way your eyes settle on the turmoil in a glass of rum. Or sharp thing the sun's become, a canticle of edges. But that's the way a trip takes place, retelling it.

One Way or Another

The hawthorn stripped, one red berry and one red leaf, the hawk's cry exhausted in your throat, an accident of flight down by the river, the jay mimicking a table saw, you slip your hand into a pocket of evidence, touch the ticket, a landscape of footprints and dark reliefs, your voice a branch repeating its leaved echoes, its wing's dark edge binding the hollow air, the body you've sketched beneath your lids, you look for the sky, vanished once again for a moment, then pirouette, drop the frayed ticket in the trash.

Espresso at Noon

He outlines the space his body fills in the shifting air, she faces him across the table, her chair resting on the yellow umbrella's fallen shade, a manhole cover sheds its microscopic splinters into the breeze above the street, she touches the outline containing an impression of him, a stranger's now though one she's almost imagined, he looks into the air's invisible substance, smudging the words that now and then escape his throat, her voice a tremolo of sounds as though she has begun to sing—a mirror in the woods, those wind chimes—

Crime

Damselflies sun themselves on a wooden rail, wind snagged in the cottonwoods, ground squirrels invading the spaces between your words, beached creatures blotching the miles of sand, a matins of birds composing their flowing patterns above the sea rising to the horizon, earth clinging to the weight of you, its momentary impressions as you walk along a road, till twilight's stars whisper against your evasions, the perfect crime you've sealed inside an envelope, hidden in the shadow of your longing.

Out and About

tubular transit   diegetic notes   waver in the backlot
    a puddle of soaking leaves   she skips across   romantic
remnants   call to the aesthete   they conspire   walk
    through clues   breathe together   bird-dotted wires
    above the alley   its musical notations spread across a
sheet of thought   as waves of rain   saturated with
    metaphor   sweep up the sidewalk   the lone ginkgo
covered with yellow   fan-shaped leaves   their autumn

Sunk City

Fingers pinned against a gate. Sunk City, its favored hues gray and black and smoke and puce. Civic attire. The stylus a tongue inscribing its exits' graffiti on the muddle we've become. A yellow bird flowering in the mud, snow flecked, slush to ash, a seasonal omen or error. Its black streaks breathe in the colors before they melt. Evade erasure mimicking night, its million streaming flakes. A yellow feather pinned to a coat, letting slip away its threadbare fabric of sun.

The Wilds

His left eye twitches   stitching off rhythms whenever the
silent signals arrive   receptors wired   birds too their
visceral patterns of flight   against the wind's collapsing
cities   a burning feather a scorched tongue   the snake's
timed articulation offbeat looking to shed its skin   but
aren't we all   *no pleasures permitted* he said *till after the*
revolution   yet a voice in the wilderness rehearsing still
backstage the circle its perfect absence   the dread at its
center

Everything and Nothing

A hanging rope   suspension bridge   arcing under
the seafarer's bethel eclipse   there   in another place
the ashes of their kingdom   a bird in the ruins   miming
the blustery weather's invisible handout   a signifying
monkey   its grifter's con calls up empty vessels
everywhere   the trickster   damp light shrouds
the forest's canopy   but in the distance a gold strip
along the sea's horizon   shedding into the troposphere

What's Left

Dreams bleeding into the mouth   lipstick smear   crayon
    cool   drool   the brutality that doesn't stop   when we
leave it behind   land mines   distempered teeth   if only
    we could dismiss all that   persists to act on our behalf

He stood between the sea and us   facing the sea   his
    head rested on the tideline   every movement a revision
a whale road   to where we were   the eyes we couldn't
    see   that saw the sea   as we thought it up   it used us
till it used us up

The fantasies we covet

of bandits roaming the out-scape, near slatted borders, no overlap, and thin columns of visible sky, through which they slip blasting paraphernalia, the volatility of their embrace caught in a dragnet of soluble light, a crow rocking a thin branch high in a tree, a kite found among the clouds, transforming their fog, the crow and its shadow rising through the fantasies of those who dream—this ambiguity becomes us, even as we're taking cover before the imagined blast.

Fevered nests

of anticipation under the white avalanche its restless
soughing before it assumes its inevitable theatrical
form and moves you enter between the pylons of
frozen air a rattled voice spilling its nonsense sentences
now mist above the snow these also their inevitable
form the earth imprinting its damaged orders across
the captured sky figures flickering at the edge
of perception vanished when you turn to inhabit them
or vanquish them their inevitable lies your rumored
lives

Strung together

after the collision of objects mistaken for birds, trees dripping orange, do you think this may be a small thing, Miles Davis in the middle register, muted, a wedding beside the waves, the long of it and the short of it, instructions along the kelp line, anxiety slipping into its coordinates, shadows staining the slope, his tilt into it a perfect angle, the plant pulled downward into the earth empties the air, the chambers of the chambers of—*smell me,* you said, again that faint promise of a smile, *smell me—*

Blue Basement

Should you wake one morning in the blue basement
Should daylight's moon faint and flattened in a story
    of endurance
dark birds darting back and forth across its sky
announce your departure all ellipses and deferral
Should rhetoric or a flight of stairs confound all effort
    in the blue basement
blue light filling every shadowed indentation in a field
    of snow you're unable to see
Should this occur and be recorded in a ledger beyond your
    calculation
Will you move to the rhythm of a premonition
remember that you *never liked stubble-fields so much as now*
    their tone and windless warmth
whisper couplets your head against a remembered breast
the you fading in the blue basement

Off

Dropped into Sight Glass for a pound or two of coffee beans to grind espresso a double to go the stairs came down carried me up to the mezzanine cup in hand caught BART past fields of rabbits and trees she wore a blue and purple dress eye shadow lipstick galactic tattoos a Celtic cross through quadrants of stars iterations stopgap the parataxis of recall some coffee roast some mezzanine what raven lift what bounce

Not a Benthic Organism to Be Seen

Your feral awareness, alien by mirth, obscures the escaping hours, night's submerged narratives, an imposition some other mind spun, scents Tom Scat the alley cat, doves fluttering up off the sidewalk, winging their complaints, their plaintive feathered notes, sunlight through your glass now, drawing on the tabletop the clear glass's transparent grays, feigning dimension

Badass

Down goat slope to ringtail river, a bullet swathed in atmosphere, that widescreen badass in the angles of your smile, zigzagging through its contending improvisations. The floor's dark surface under an insect's four translucent fanned-out wings. Lyle would love it, hair piled on top of hair, loose summer dress, splotches of blue and rose on white. Do you still have that ability to float motionless above the floor, with longer shadows now dimming the day?

FOUR

So walk on air against your better judgement
—Seamus Heaney, "The Gravel Walks"

Cucumber Slumber

The title of a piece by Weather Report

You dip a finger into a trickle   of consciousness
conscience   the knowing of it   trace the zero's
emptiness   your breath fills   incognito in any crowd
for one more day   favored by light   you step out
through the door   arguing with the indifferent air
your adrenaline sanctioned   your one ticket validated
by trail and terror   out of the past   a vibraphone
rainstorm   the body's Euphrates of the mountains
residuum under a flurry of forgotten words   and now
you just want to learn   how to sleep standing up
in the field   like a horse

π

Mosquito island
aromas and bites
on Spider river

lick me
you said
but slowly
lap me up

pick the pickup
up here

I want to be a pickup
picked up

near the used literature
π's timeless flow

the island
spiders frozen
the river's thin
surface iced

Transparent animals

afloat in harmonies of our Houdini
walk along a sea wall, transparent too

glass buildings mirror the sky
disappear in their reflections

a whispered kiss tests the quiet fugitive
una furtiva lagrima
as stories burn

the mapped trail winding itself a pattern
cherry bark and large, soft birds

those small halogen insects inside the brain externalized
resting on the air

She's Singing for You

Her dress of many colors   opals of sound   through
pastoral sheens of greening glass   a torch singer's glittery
trim   slinky and black   wind-chimed   stop time
under a gust's incurable path   and dross the singer
sifts through   leaf drift to slake her thirst   beyond
the castle's rain-streamed walls   forever
under construction

Swamp Music

The daemon in the neural works   *sabotexteur*
    deconstructs the symbolic maze   t r e e s   t u r n
m i g r a t e   animals begin their travels across the
    dissonant waves of sound   the citadel just out of reach
its sandstone alphabets   returned to sand   salt lick
    sentinels under its tongue   fields moving   under eddies
of granular mist.   turtle mouth   slits open a face   slips
    out at night   as swamp music   ignites the fungal
underworld

Commotion

El alma inflable the owl in the sutures and hanged him
by the numbers as blood reentered the hangman's arm
bearing a nice sting to it a daydreamed sun that fanned
her hair abrasive embraces the tableau black tile with
skittering silverfish like dim sum setting tissued
wings aflutter setting flustered wings ablaze
stakeout those invisible ports burst into waves
of intimation palm to sea's circumference *una tormenta*
against their shores

Frequency Hopping

Hedy Lamarr's term for spread spectrum radio technology

    step over a fractured i-beam becoming mist   into the
woods   steel blue in the fogged light   impose the city's
    grid over its duff   to count out components of time

    that green bird lost in your hair   among its green
the way we stepped into space   the air burst   pulling us
into the slipstream   blood on the frost under your tongue
    or fire the yellow jacket   left in your mouth   its poison
mixed with the sugary drink

    we walked the causeway   sat under the sea   our image
fallow   in the fading sky   our voice engorged
    with sea light

Jump

A moody wind   smears the mountain to abstraction
a flâneur idle on a beach of drifting sand
weed tips restless in their burial   disfiguring the dunes

an assassin in his own right   ice biting the palm
of his hand   composing this

there is no such thing   as neutral space

a goldfinch sat on his hat   slept in a box   aboard
a boat   woke up and flew away   water on the move

with attitude   will he be there   when it arrives
that howling in the distance   beyond the mountain's
memory   will he sense it   catch its scent
before it jumps

?

He sometimes turns into a question mark   with help
from the sheriff's machete   a disruptive curve and point
that opens a door   the wall beyond the door a sheet
of glaring light   she enters through   an emanation
source or second disruption   relief from the light
and he less focused   in the present tense

Remember below the snow line   we walked among
the dogwoods   in blossom   I don't do you   remember that
I sometimes turn into a question mark   You have she said
a bass note swam behind the wall   the consistency
of blood   subsumed their words   *Could you take on some*
other mark   ? he said   her voice lost in the throbbing air

Chinese Umbrella

A bright red Chinese umbrella
eyelid of wind
disturbs those plates
of light in the leaves
where the wolf
incognito waits

a head visible at low tide
final acknowledgment
of disrepair
the bloodied blade reflected
in a blade of thought

street noise for a mockingbird's
inebriation
while bats comb
their lustrous fur

a finger of fine
sandpaper
across your Braille
that weeping willow
hairdo a multitude
of moving parts
below an indecipherable
swerve of sky

An insect's narrative

crosses the page
    the shortest distance
between two stars
    or this many fingers

A light year of lingering consequence
    the small wind scattering notations of bliss

He sped along a dark road
in every version
    a familiar road
though one he wouldn't recognize

I remember what we saw
what we imagined
    in wells of light

The alarm gone off beside his bed
    a purple sound
persistent in invisible layers
of soft white glass

Give Me One Reason

Title of a song by Tracy Chapman

I need an accelerant to light up   but not ignite   our
    snapshot negative   afloat on a riptide under the bridge

    our demon brother has just left   his chrysalis
hanging in a tree   that fog bank over your heart   that
    hedgehog in mine   remember that appetite for insects
or appetite in sex   prickly I know   the crow's face
    a blank page   a plum in its beak

    feel the wind picking up in the crevices   a contrition
all around   *ground down*   *worn away*   *rubbed together*
    polished stone for what remains   if we must   let's
come apart

The tenacity of failed escapes

we spoke of once
I want you, I thought

I heard you say

An army of insects
locusts, *moscas*, who knew the names

Layers of skin where ink lives, splinters
toxins or parasites move

That rank perfume left in a room

Your marginal observations criminally acclaimed
nets of indecision, they too were fabled

A carousel of discordant beliefs
wished away

Touch me, I thought

Umbrellas suspended like bandits in baskets of steel

High wire in the wind

Thomas Tallis

after Janet Cardiff's Forty Part Motet *sound installation*

A voice in a box   each boxed in   in the wind's interiors
surrounding us

an osprey lost in Farsi   nesting numbers   fish fed

that shade that runs through our veins   seeps
into cavities   helter-skelter   immaterial though it is
scratches

the water steel green   cloud troubled   cut with light
the coroner our crooner

that hydroplane   its scar drawn across the Sound

your motet's many voices   gathered us in their
transcendent embrace   suspended a garden's dissonance
its hanging spiders colluding there

FIVE

One story is good till another is told.

—Aesop proverb

The Park

I phone-shoot our hungry intimacy in the fading light. Do it, he said. Afterward we vibrate in the night. Words are coming out of his mouth. I lean down, feel their warmth against my face, salty, a lingering hum of sex, listen instead to a current running beneath.

I roll off onto my back. The smoke alarm's small bead of blinking light moves across the dark ceiling and doesn't move. A loud voice, angry and belligerent, in the alley, or park just across the street, suddenly occupies the room. I close my ears and let the ocean wash over the words—the voice a whirlpool of broken things.

We open the door. Morning. Light sent out in every direction, last night's voice stunned in the sunlight. We trace it, find him in the park, give him a little something to quiet the earth. He glances up, catches my eye—s'all good, girl—and we're on our way.

Ice

I picture now your powder-blue gown, or was it my own jacket, a powder-blue rental, resisting a quickening pulse, the falling dark. Maybe a dance we might have attended in some inelegant perfumed hotel. Flakes of shredded paper, phrases forgotten, fill a knapsack left in the snow. We work our way up the rippled surface of a frozen stream, unknown flocks swirling through the hesitant blue. Bare iced branches and brambles enclose the stream, the ice receding behind us, breaking up as it reaches the sea, fish sleeping beneath our feet, dreaming of rough currents folding in the light.

Dream Catcher

I thought that you could find us in the dark, our rabbit-skin hats against the frost. We did place the idols upright in a doorway. And hid in our nakedness, white among the leaves. Maybe we were mistaken for an illusion, our voice left in the spectacle. So dark once I almost swallowed a spider, confused and scratching the surface in a cup of water. Would it have spun contrivances in the soul? The dream catcher brought us here, and we were full of anticipation. But you uttered the curse, and then some apparition murdered its double. The elixir it sought concealed in the blood. The vapors we've thought into imagery! Brown helicopters flying in tandem—large insects moving across the sky—

Body Blur

You disappear a fog into another body, blur its supple outline. What's left of you an incoming tide of chords, afterimage, spent breath.   Who to whom   am I speaking   to   now?   A mouthful of sound, snow spray against a face, crocus up through the snow, daffodils or some yellow outburst. Wings that make visible the wind. All part of the days we've passed.

Night's vibrations holding us in an aura of flying bugs. We cross the lawn, swat away the air we dream. Silver letters shimmering against the dark, flow down its dark screen in rivulets a cryptic storm.

The Whale

after the children's story El caballito de siete colores

Talk to me, the whale said, under the bridge. Would you bring me a cappuccino and something sweet, an almond or chocolate biscotti, and we will sing a whale's song to bagpipes and flute, and praise the wonder of jicama with just a pinch of spice.

As the water rises I will swim out to sea, the bridge on my back, and *you* if you dare. The bridge in time will break apart and wash ashore and scatter its remnants across the beach. And we will dive beneath the waves and dance our dance in the depths of the sea.

Woodshedding

A late neon magenta sun
the fires have lit

In damp shadows a thousand flies
swarm your face

Lost in the rural expanses of your body
mower blades and cut hay
nourishing the wind

Woodshedding
in search of a theme
some transubstantiation

The bell in the tower
threatening the air
inserts itself among the notes

Sleepers awake

Hawk light
its shadow for an instant above its prey
whose ghost already inhabits its talons and wings

While Philomela
locked in a shed
weaves our crimes
into a breathing tapestry

The Book

We find our way
through a book of last laments

toward a transparent tower
(whose outline we see)

become a green pasture of sheep and ruins

lying in the mist just beyond
the tower balanced

at the edge of thought

We forge through the text
ford a river's shallows

its language slipping beneath us
distance feeding on its own extension

A diagonal light
ascends the horizon

A drop of light
slides down a bowl's inner surface

the cowrie bowl you cup in your palm
as patches of shadow

dissolve on your face
the bowl you carry an offering

to those voices we imagine
the walls of the tower becoming

as we come to the tower

The Care of Wounds

He tries to spend time
in a world where she still exists
a land of vanishing birds and ice

He cuts open a seam in the air
to slip through
cauterizes her image to keep it
from bleeding away

He remembers the cold
after she was gone
coming off her absence
her ghost stretched out next to him

One day she sat on a wooden bench
outside a café
her back to the window

Bringing out their coffee
he noticed a small decal on the glass
a blue snowflake

printing its icy image
on the back of her neck
a pattern he imagined

grazing the tide
of living
and expired stars

Notes

"Looking for the Car": Alki is a beach on Puget Sound in West Seattle.

"Fable": The inscription *El puente es tuyo* ("The bridge is yours") appears above a footbridge in La Peñita, Mexico.

Epigraph, Part Two: From *Longitude* (London: Fourth Estate, 1996).

"Isfahan": "Isfahan is half of the world" is a seventeenth-century Persian proverb inspired by the city's beauty.

Epigraph, "Ashes": From *Library of Dust* (San Francisco: Chronicle Books, 2008).

Epigraph, Part Three: San Francisco Opera produced Antonin Dvořák's *Rusalka* in 2019. The quotation is from one of the arias sung by the title character. Christopher Bergen translated the Czech libretto for this production.

"Out and About": The word *diegetic* means "happening within the created world of a story."

"What's Left": "Whale road" (*hron-rāde*) is an Old English kenning for "sea." It appears in *Beowulf*, line 10, translation by Seamus Heaney (New York: Farrar, Straus and Giroux, 2000).

"Blue Basement": "I never liked stubble-fields so much as now" appears in a letter John Keats wrote to J. H. Reynolds.

Epigraph, Part Four: From *The Spirit Level: Poems* (New York: Farrar, Straus and Giroux, 1996). "Walk on air against your better judgement" appears on Heaney's headstone.

"Cucumber Slumber": From *Mysterious Traveller* (New York: Sony and Columbia, 1974).

"Transparent Animals": The well-known aria *Una furtiva lagrima* ("A furtive tear") is from Gaetano Donizetti's comic opera *The Elixir of Love.*

"Commotion": *El alma inflable* ("The inflatable soul"); *una tormenta* ("a storm").

"Frequency Hopping": Spread spectrum, a WW2 radio technology that Hedy Lamarr helped develop, was used to disrupt the German tracking of torpedoes heading toward their ships.

"Jump": "There is no such things as neutral space" is from the British Iraqi architect Zaha Hadid.

"Give Me One Reason": From *New Beginnings* (New York: Elektra, 1995).

"Thomas Tallis": For her *Forty Part Motet* sound installation, Janet Cardiff recorded Tallis's *Spem in alium (*"Hope in any other"*)* with the Salisbury Cathedral Choir, each singer with his own mic, then divided the forty speakers into groups of five and arranged the eight groups in a circle. Listeners could move around, listening to individual singers, a group, or the entire choir.

“The Whale”: The images of the whale and the bridge, though not the narrative, are from the children’s story *El caballito de siete colores* from *Cuentos que contaban nuestras abuelas* (New York: Simon & Schuster, 2006).

“Woodshedding”: “Sleepers Awake” is the English name for Johann Sebastian Bach’s Cantata BWV 140, *Wachet auf, ruft uns die Stimme* (“Wake up, the voice calls to us”). Philomela was a princess in Greek mythology. Assaulted by her sister’s husband, who cut out her tongue and imprisoned her to keep her from revealing what he had done, she wove an account of his crime into a tapestry. Ovid tells her story in *Metamorphoses*.

Acknowledgments

Many thanks to the editors of the following publications, in which these poems first appeared, some in different versions:

Aji: "The Whale," "Fable," "Flood," "Thomas Tallis"; *Angry Old Man*: "Swamp Music," "The fantasies we covet," "Give Me One Reason," "Frequency Hopping," "Cucumber Slumber"; *Club Plum*: "To the Water's Edge"; *Doorknobs & BodyPaint*: "Saddle Up"; *Eclectica Magazine*: "Frogs in the Basement"; *Fleas on the Dog*: "π," "Fevered nests," "Dream Catcher," "Ashes," "Espresso at Noon"; *Hole in the Head*: "One Way or Another"; *Into the Void* (Ireland): "What are you looking for"; *I-70 Review*: "The Care of Wounds"; *LAdige*: "Birds," "If I wake up falling"; *Otoliths*: "Sunk City," "Body Blur," "The Wilds," "Strung together," "Everything and Nothing," "Out and About"; *Permafrost*: "Isfahan"; *Poetalk*: "An insect's narrative," "There's No One Here"; *Poetry Flash*: "Dear Sara," "Departure," "Looking for the Car," "Fable"; *Riverbabble*: "Frequencies"; *Subprimal*: "Doubt"; *VOLT*: "Commotion."

"?" was published in the anthology *The Other Side of Violet* (Great Weather for MEDIA).

Sixteen Rivers Press is a shared-work, nonprofit poetry collective dedicated to providing an alternative publishing avenue for Northern California poets. Founded in 1999 by seven writers, the press is named for the sixteen rivers that flow into San Francisco Bay.

SAN JOAQUIN • FRESNO • CHOWCHILLA • MERCED • TUOLUMNE
STANISLAUS • CALAVERAS • BEAR • MOKELUMNE • COSUMNES
AMERICAN • YUBA • FEATHER • SACRAMENTO • NAPA • PETALUMA